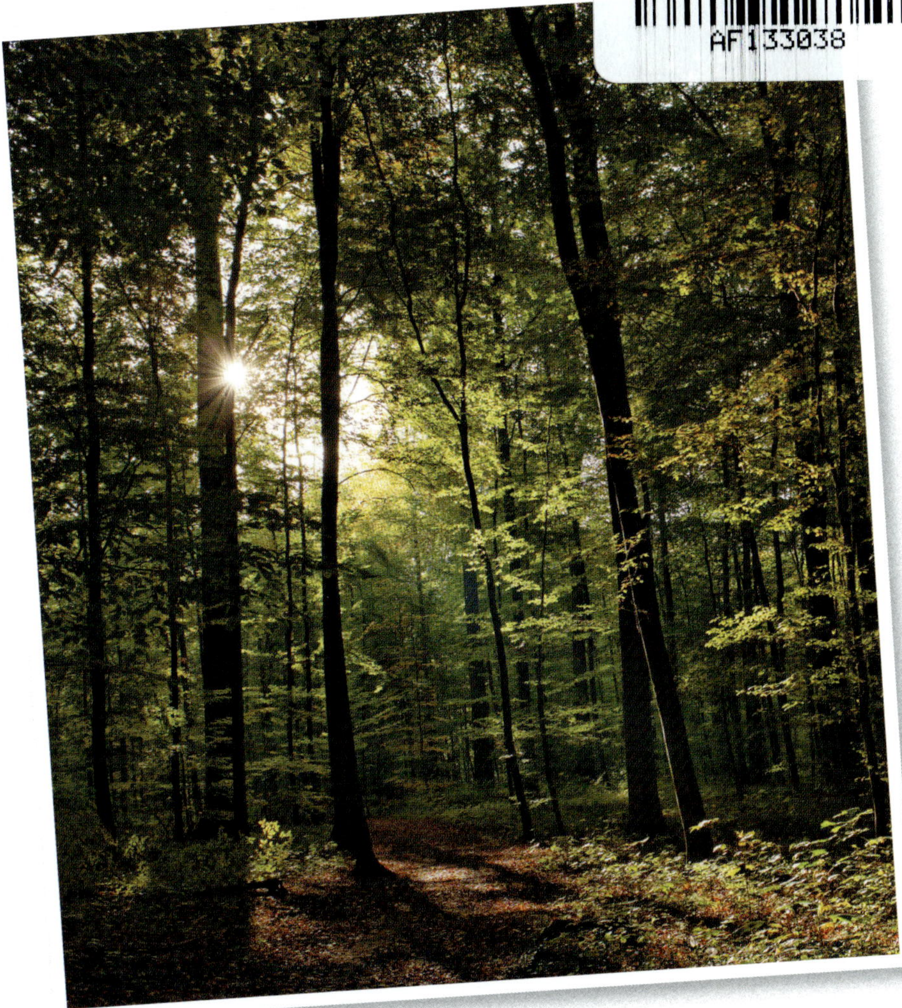

In the forest

we see...

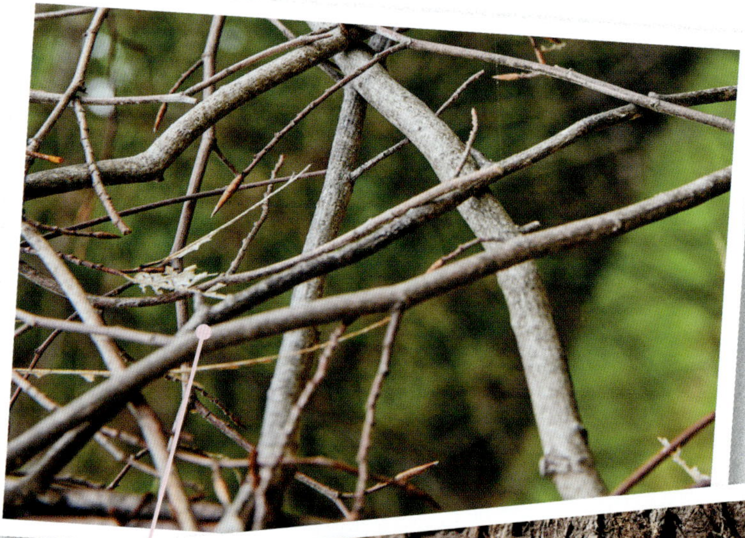

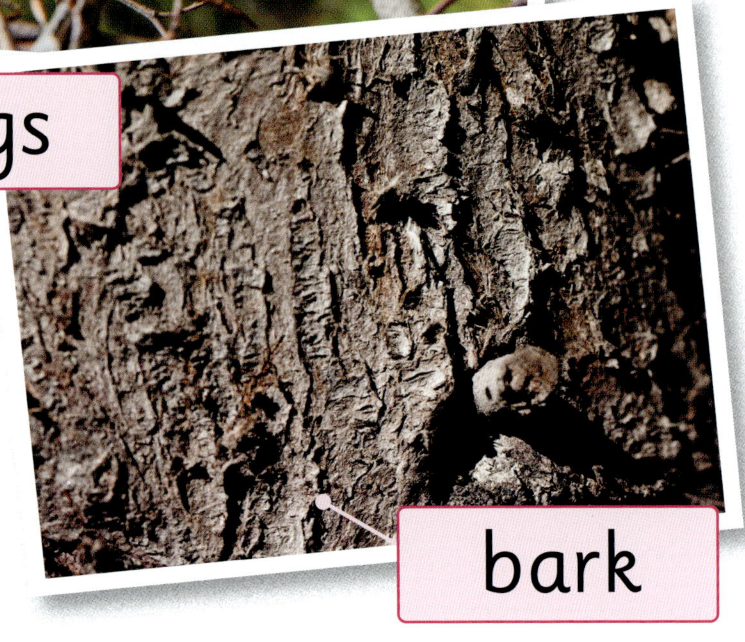

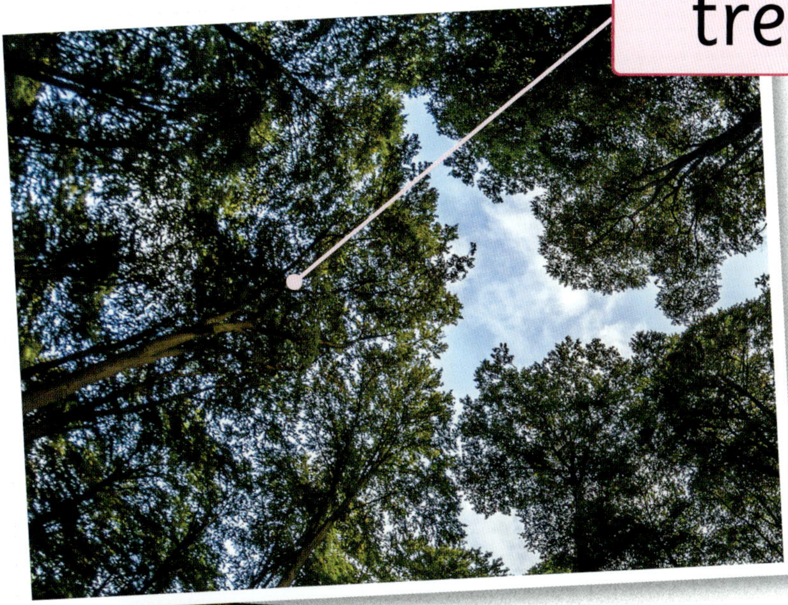
trees

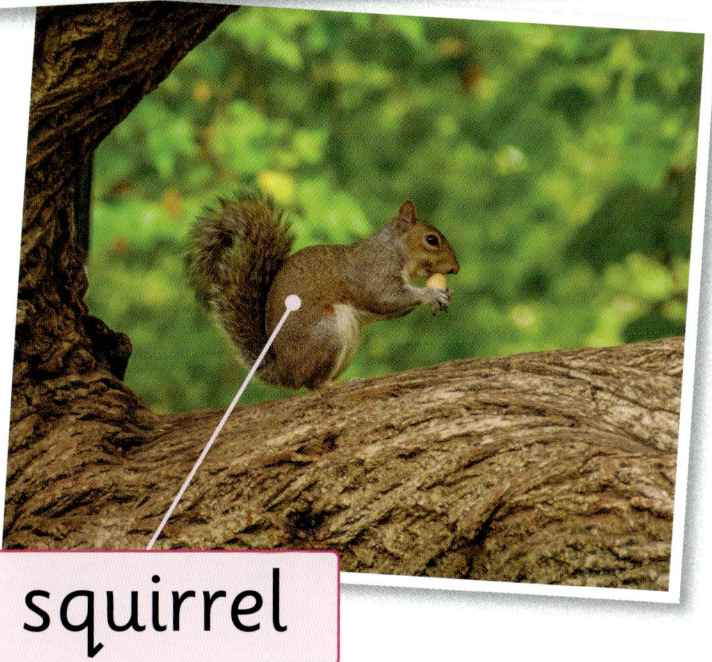
a squirrel

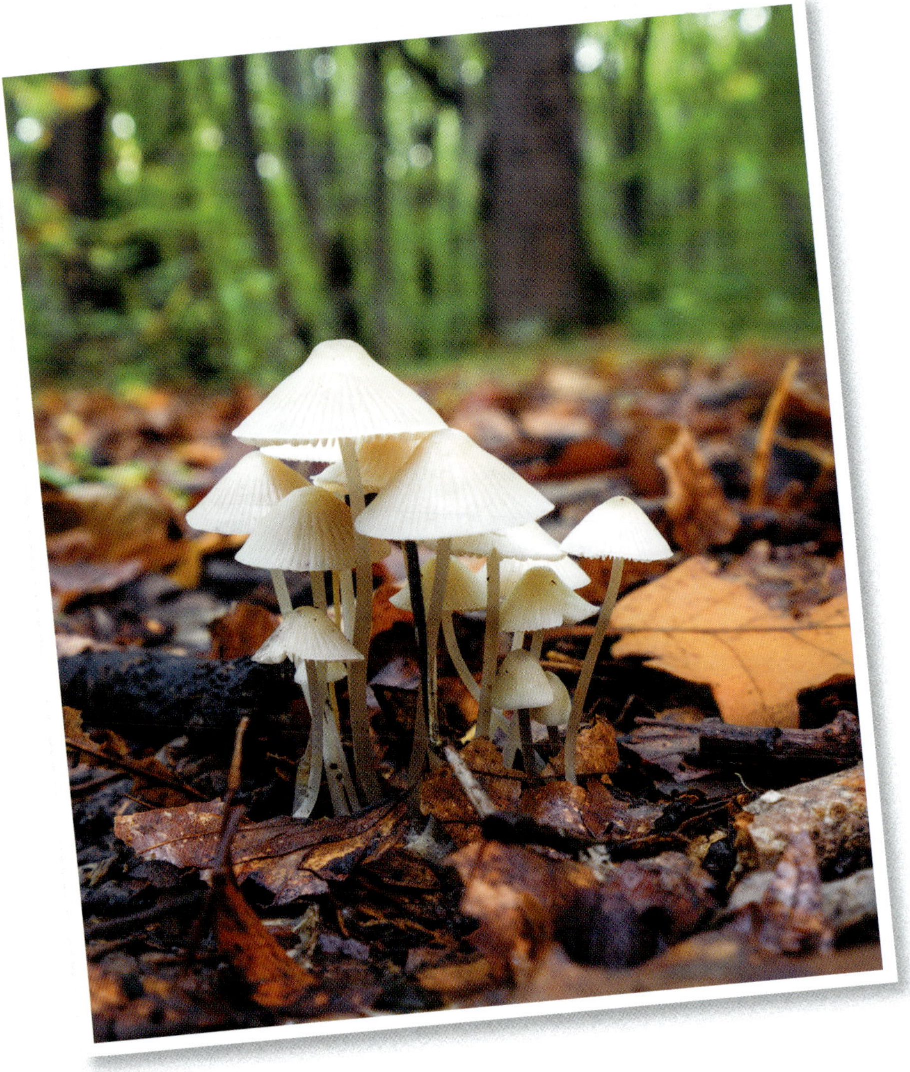

mushrooms

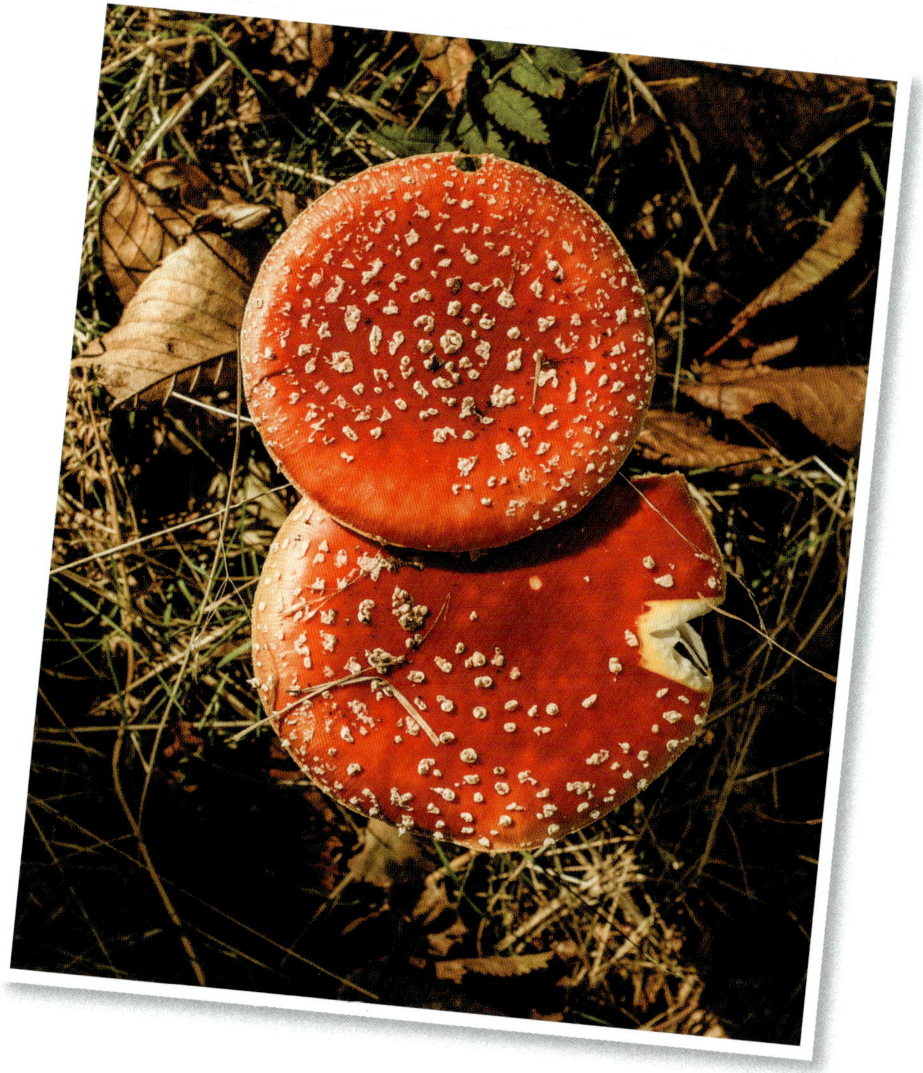

and toadstools.

This is a log.

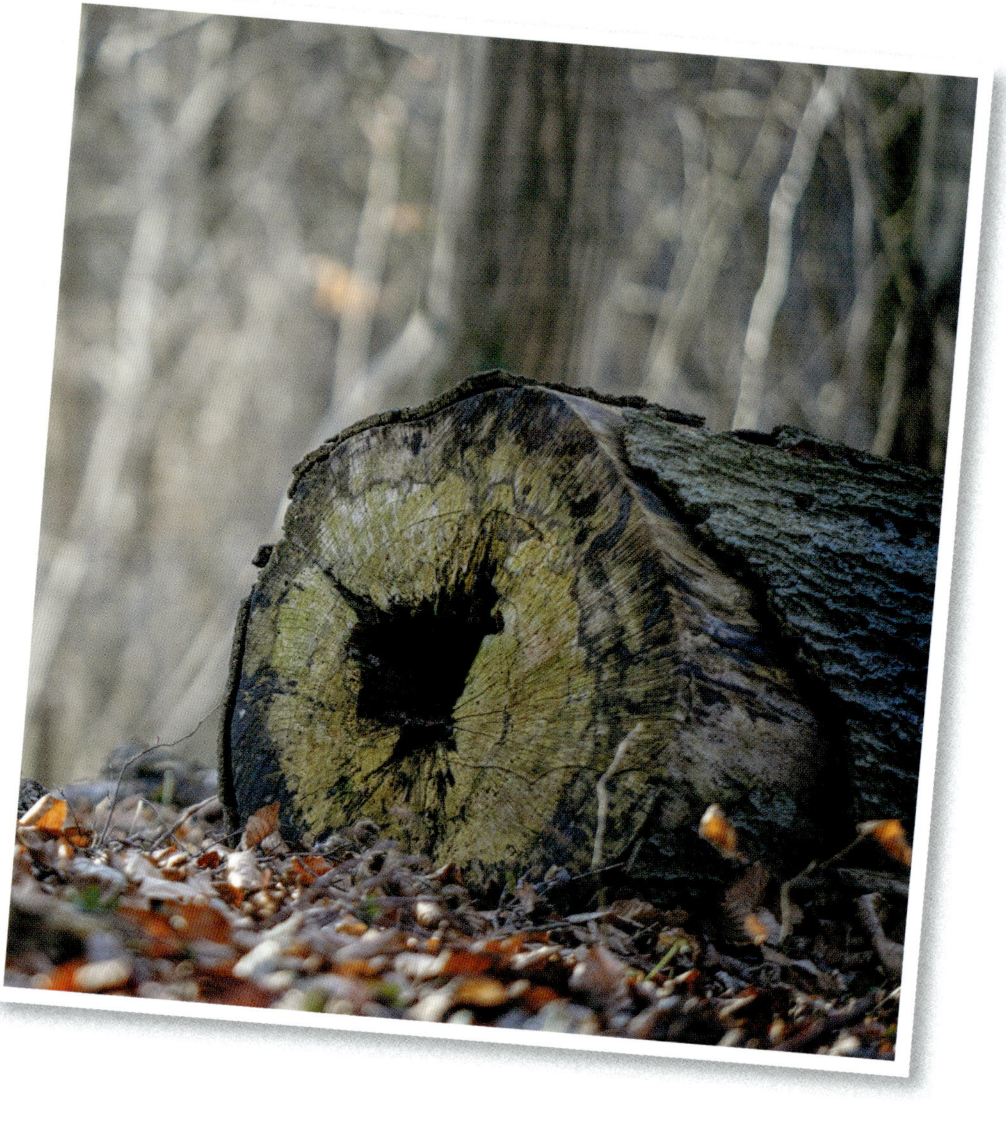

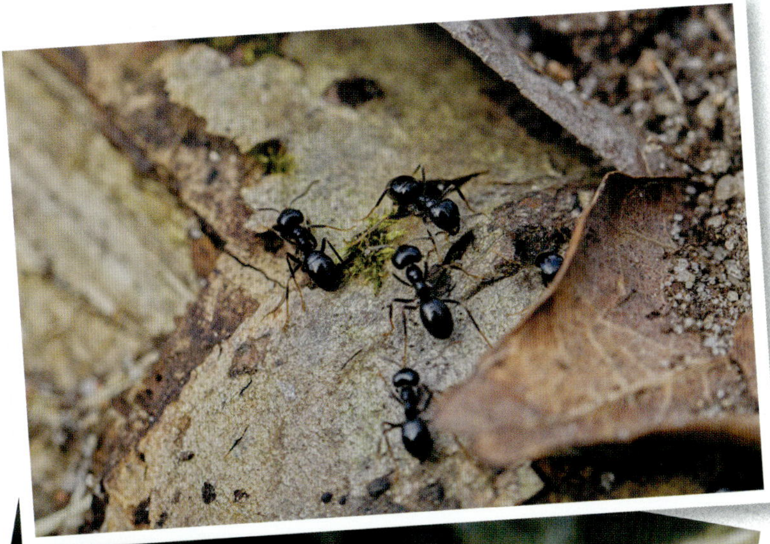

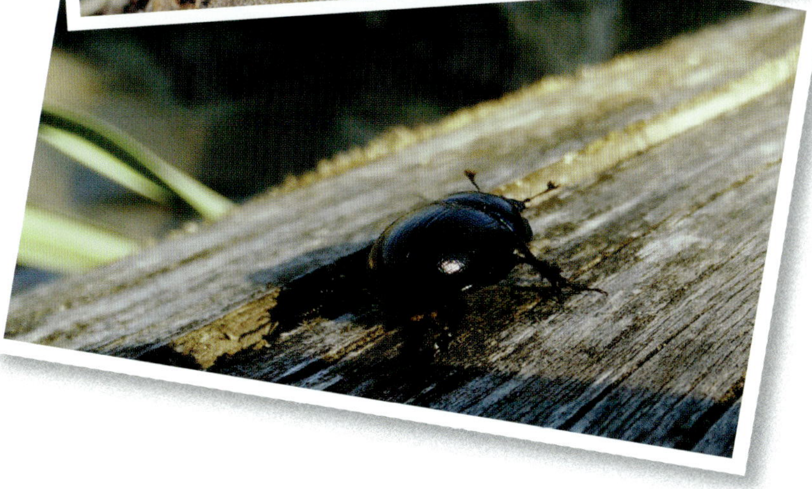

Spot the bugs
on it...

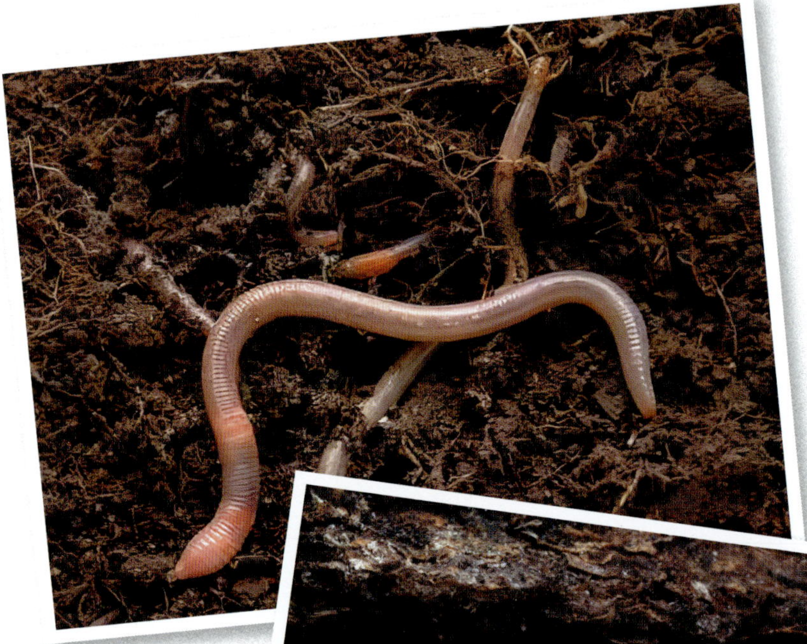

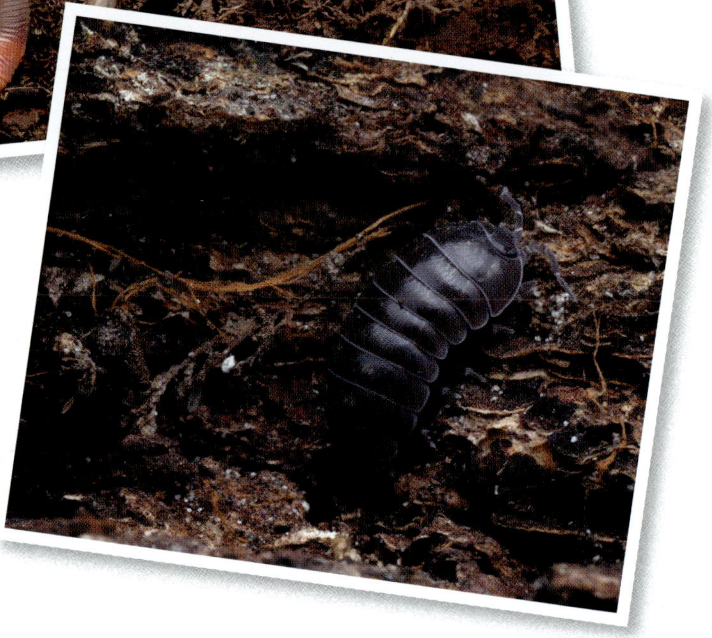

and under it!